salmonpoetry

Celebrating 35 Years
of Literary Publishing

Ghost of the Fisher Cat

Afric McGlinchey

For Marion —
Thanks for a memorable
evening — for everything.
Warmest — Afric pp
12.10.17 Belfast.

Published in 2016 by
Salmon Poetry
Cliffs of Moher, County Clare, Ireland
Website: www.salmonpoetry.com
Email: info@salmonpoetry.com

ISBN 978-1-910669-39-6

FRONT COVER: *Altered photograph, design and typesetting by Michael Ray,
based on a mural which has been attributed to Némo*
BACK COVER DESIGN & TYPESETTING: *Siobhán Hutson*
Printed in Ireland by Sprint Print

*Salmon Poetry gratefully acknowledges the support of
The Arts Council / An Chomhairle Ealaoín*

and the shadows grew denser

more visible and solid than the real things

–Edvin Sugarev

Acknowledgements

Acknowledgements are due to the editors of the following publications in which versions of some of these poems have appeared: *Abridged, Ambit, De Profundis* (an anthology of poems written in response to Oscar Wilde's *De Profundis*, published by Sybaratic Press in USA), *Dublin Poetry Review, Feeling the Heat* (Trocaire and Poetry Ireland anthology), *Lost Between* (an anthology published in Italian by Guanda and in English by New Island), *New Mirage* (USA), *Numéro Cinq, O Bhéal* anthology, *Poetry Ireland Review, Shot Glass Journal, Sixteen, Southword, The Brain of Forgetting, The Lion Tamer Dreams of Office Work* (anthology, published by Alba), *The SHOp, The Stinging Fly, Uimhir a Cúig, Writers' Hub*.

A version of 'I Is Not Always Me' won the 2015 Poets Meet Politics competition. A version of 'Dinner in Nine Movements' was Editors' Choice for the 2012 Northern Liberties Prize. Versions of 'Pareidolia' and 'Sonnet in B Major' were highly commended in the 2014 and 2015 O Bhéal poetry competitions. 'Slow Dancing in a Burning Room' was runner up in the Trócaire poetry competition 2015.

For their invaluable insights, my grateful thanks to Eileen Sheehan, John Fitzgerald, John Mee and my much appreciated critical readers at UCC's poetry workshop. Thanks also to my non-poet friend, Jane Skovgaard, ('I love having my opinion sought'), and my son, Cian Hamilton, for their generous input. My love and gratitude, especially, to Michael Ray, whose presence in my life is an endless inspiration. And Micaela, my daughter, who makes me so proud.

I am also grateful for the sustaining support of Patrick Cotter and the Munster Literature Centre, Paul Casey, founder of Cork's renowned O Bhéal series, and the Irish Writers' Centre, who selected me for an Italo-Irish Writers' Exchange. Most importantly, I would like to thank my wonderful publisher, Jessie Lendennie and the endlessly patient and brilliant Siobhán Hutson.

Thanks also to Cork County Council for awarding me an arts bursary and to Uillinn: West Cork Arts Centre, for a four-month residency.

CONTENTS

Familiar

Cat Music

A drownling is lifted
from a rain barrel,

dark as a slick of oil;
stripped with a blade,

organs separated
from fat and manure,

soaked overnight
in alkaline water;

scraped once more,
then stirred

through sulfuric fumes;
rolled into elongated

strings; attached
to an instrument

and tuned; ready
for horsehair to stroke

into music so intricate
and astonishing,

you would think
the animal had arisen.

Souvenir

To let fingers trail railings, abseil
padlocks on the Pont des Artes;

to see girls splayed on a river
bench, their vintage dresses,

hand on a thigh, tongues slipping
in-and-out, over gloss;

to stretch bare arms from wall to wall
across the Rue du Chat qui Pêche,

to eat a *crêpe de sucre de citron*;
count the bells' *ding dong, ding dong*;

to hear gunfire heels along
the cobblestones of Rue Mouffetard –

is to feel the strings of the city pulling
me back, to relocate. Recollect.

Vital Impulse

'I have a cat now. It comes in, it goes out.'
—Matthew Hollis

He can't sit still.
Kept in too long,
and he's up and down
with the incomprehensible
leapings of a branded creature.
He walks very fast,
vibrations casting bait
in various directions.
Not that I'm saying he's hunting.

It's just that, in this state,
he's unreachable,
as though an invisible glass
surrounds his agile body.
At other times,
I could walk
right through him.
All matter is merely
image, after all.

In any case, he isn't there,
but squalling
on some rooftop,
or springing from the highest tree,
his only landing gear,
ingenuity.
The best approach
is an open door.
He eventually comes in.

Familiar

'This Dom Perlet. Who is he, really?
In spite of the cassock and sermons,
he's put it about that he's an apothecary –
my own mother came home with blue cohosh!
Look – there's his cat! Have you observed how
they walk through the city, uncannily close,
as though figure and shadow? Or witch and familiar!
Madame Flotté, who lost her tenth baby?
She visited him. There's proof he's a sorcerer.
That firecracker cat, his eyes – blazing curses?
Let's burn it! A death fit for a diabolist intimate.
Remember Jeanne d'Arc, whose charred
bones were disposed of, in this very river?

Better still, let's drown it. That's easier.
For our neighbours, a favour, *n'est-ce pas?*
Look how the feline curves its ears backward,
spooning sound from behind it – is it listening?
What's more, there's something infernal in the way
each scoop of its paw hooks a shad from the river!
Let's approach slowly; but beware of those claws –
it's a war-cat when cornered. I tried, once before,
set fire to its tail. But the monster leapt twenty
feet high, then dived into the Seine! I swear
it was witchery. We all know cats hate to swim –
but I'm telling you, it weaved like an eel!
We must hold the sack down until it stops moving.
Hey! Don't look at me! Aren't you following?'

1606 Round-Up

'May you always have hope'
    – blessing offered on the street

Fog shrouds the Cimitière des Innocents.
My ears begin to hurt; too late
to back out now. I blunder forward,
after others, breathing out
small clouds. To follow, or be left?
I am ten years older
than the boy who landed.

Blazing torches on the deck
hurl ghosts and shadows.
Shame of the journey home,
empty-handed! Behind me, the city
is all bone and smoke.
I receive rations; lumber
up the gangway, into a wailing past.

Down below, thin blankets, unraveled
dirty bandages. Next to me, the intrusion
of a presence. I think of other perils,
like loneliness and demons.
As warmth begins to seep across the district
of the bunks, I grasp my mother's periapt,
take back a whispered Irish curse.

Night's Three Faces

I

Cats compose the dark, wrapped
in the weight of night devilment.
They chew on the tale of a quay of flames,
fire-sister, mutable skies.
There is violence too, in the camber
of voices around the weight of indiscretions.
Cars reverse like a tongue.
A snake cloud. So much to hide.
Every night, the kingdom comes.

II

The lyric river is calling,
as if the word 'fog' were full of groping shadows.
Rain in the dark, harmonic.
Birds gather oil, sticky and slow.
One flicks up a clot that clips a man cycling
past us, as we sit cocooned in a hot car on the pier.
How long can a drowning cat
struggle in a hessian sack?
But this is just a long night in a room.

III

Trees bucking, throwing their limbs to the sky,
full of the lungs of a two-year-old girl
hoisted on to a father's shoulders,
seeing the world from that towering height.
From here, forests
can foretell their own forced breath
filled with the sting of a chainsaw.
I've spent so many hours streaking past
the screaming silence packed below me.

Spirit Level

Below the quay, where the evening air barely stirs,
lads lean against the slimy wall, boots rooted in the muck.
There's a rite. He daren't give lip. They make him
drink litres, till he's lost as a pilot in fog.

The off-licence keeper sighs, takes down the fliers
promoting the previous night's concert.
He waits for his wife to slope past him,
mop up the slop left by the late night revelers.

Like oil spilt on a garage floor after a day's toil, there's peril
for each pedestrian piloting around the spoilt pavement.
She drags out a bucket, jostles the warm, soapy water.
Plop. Before the day's out, someone slips on it.

The bats are the only witnesses.
From crevices, spores wait for air, like pores
on the skin of a boy, lying, face down
in the silt, hair stiff as a brush.

Confluence

His manner is reserved,
a little secretive.
He scours the room, which also pines
for colour; moves
to the window's blazing snap of light.

Her age depends on the light,
especially the collarbone's
slight hollow at the V,
a wishbone, which gives luck
only when broken.

He is both still and moving,
like a tree in the trembling
haul of spring,
building up its nests
and growing puddles.

She spends the water
with spread fingers.
He is afraid of loss –
it's easier to have nothing.
No way in for the water; no way out.

It's herself she's in danger from,
seizing a handful of electric wire,
as though clutching-
for-dear-life
a hank of drowning hair.

He paints what's left behind.
A thought-ghost grieves,
disturbed by mutation;
like seeing the bones of tiny,
once-swimming fish.

She notes there's no
fountain swishing,
only light.
Weightlessness
encloses her.

They share a reading
of each other's bodies
among the hung-up coats,
mud-sucked boots;
the track.

She looks up to find
the sky wiped free
of the drench;
his voice shifting
to a minor key.

Fête des Trépassés

Like mountain air raked suddenly
by a drop in temperature, flesh is stirred
where no flesh decks the bones.

The river churns as centuries of spirits
lift from buried sacks
and flow above its lovers' bridges.

Two skim across the dimly-green jardins,
perennial familiars. 'In fantasies,
you crushed me, like a blossom in your fist!'

Next to the obelisk, they pass
the white illumination of a giant Ferris wheel.
Though it's still, they take a ride.

Spectres cluster in the square at St Germain,
one busking, 'Love me Two Times'.
A pale density of dancers.

In the empty shadow-city, our couple
drifts along the cobble-stones,
past mausoleums, weeping statues.

'And now, my Héloïse?' he asks, and she responds,
'Men called me chaste. What a hungry hypocrite
I was. Come, Pierre, unknot me!'

He draws a breath of frost, lifts her plaited rope
of phantom hair and looses it. She merges into particles;
remembers flesh and bone and kiss.

All Souls' air is flimmering but,
though an owl flits past, his yellow eye on them,
neither death nor hell can trespass.

A River of Familiars

I have a cat that sharpens her scent on men.
    I netted her from the river, called her mother.

Perhaps there's a cat-flap in the sky,
    because sometimes my mother's a golden owl.

I have a memory cat that in a past life
    knew the taste of golden whiskey.

My cat has a curiosity about the whiskey-crazy
    wish for public nudity.

I have a crazy city cat with a lightning dart
    across her lazy eye.

And my lightning cat has an earring, just the one,
    mother-of-pearl. Call it intuition.

And seven secret positions, the last
    a chanting lotus. I have a cat that doesn't exist.

I have a penchant for jumping trains, inhaling
    with each knock. I have a sister cat who inhales too.

I have a lover who becomes a lion under the glassy moon.
    And the cat exhales her wail, like an accordion.

One cat is a grand, glass-lidded, gleaming ivory,
    the light not yet put out.

First-born, I am, of a cat who cycles lightly
    inside his mansion full of stories, war and music.

My cat and I wear twenty masks when singing
    out in rain, take it, like a wafer, on the tongue.

I have a cat that purrs in white and black
or foggy smoke rings, belly up.

As a foggy curtain rises, a missing cat
runs rings around the time inside a clock.

Slow Dancing
in a Burning Room

Leap

Let's say a cat
leaps
and I follow,
lifting my feet, the way
my sister taught me,
into the big bang
of first love.

I am soaring,
then land,
soft as a cat,
on a red-brick ledge,
among African violets,
his hands on a pair
of newly-found

planets;
then a mouth
cruising skin,
hatching a nipple;
so blushingly unexpected,
I burn
for decades.

Dinner in Nine Movements

Al claims his space with gestures,
neglecting our hostess, who falters
when she sees his skinny, laughing wife;
flaps, like a flag recovering from a squall.

And so the conversation passes, like a dish
around the table; Flossie's eyes downcast,
as though to make her own largesse invisible.
Kurt, fresh from his circuit – square, chateau and hill –

pours expensive wine; nods modestly
as his haute cuisine is praised. And round it goes,
the talk of pain relief and aftermath, speculation about
a god, unknowable anxieties and efforts to control.

A tiny bell of iron in Al's voice; and when I boast
about our hen, who lays an egg each day, he asks
if I'm as fertile, glances back and forth between us,
and pointedly, at my yellow cocktail dress.

Calls my fella a 'cool cat'. They, of course, are casual
chic. Diane's mignon, fine boned and delicate,
bob sleek and swinging; older than me. Al lays
a hand across her knee; she doesn't seem to notice.

Her eyes are trained on my cool cat, talking
about his gran, who once visited this very chateau;
stared, stricken, at a wing that wasn't there.
It had burnt down centuries before.

She saw two red-robed figures at a window,
swept up in the flames. And now I detect it too,
the burning. We skirt around hallucinatory smells,
psychosis, strange workings of the mind.

Flossie's hands are folded in her lap, diminishing.
Kurt, picking up the cue, lifts a decanter, pours
splashingly. On a screen through an open doorway,
Esperanza Spalding, descending métro steps,

a cello on her back. Against curved, graffitied walls,
she draws a bow across the strings.
As one, we turn to her: those in the métro,
the dinner party guests; perhaps, some ghosts.

Portrait of the Other

Like art (an addiction,
not a cure), you're

the moonlit flit from
silk to gold, to wings

to glass; light as cats,
and sniper-accurate;

a heliotropic paradox
facing five horizons.

You're a pack of jokers,
deuces, three-eyed queens;

the immensity of an
ocean or inferno;

you're a shadow-grue,
sunlight and lawn,

and all the time
in the world.

Frescoes

We were skilled at being criminals.
Any closed structures were open sesame.
We crammed walls with our soliloquies:
my skinny girls, their liquorice eyes;
your crimson galleon sails.
The cloister of dark where we discovered African masks,
and those firecrackers fountaining the sky in yellows
and greens on bonfire night;
the electric tension when you took my hand
before the rest arrived to squat, stare into the river.
And that was that. Our moment stolen.

I've squirreled all of it:
the cobbled alleys with forget-me-nots,
the way we scattered when someone spotted us;
the orchid you once stole through a left-open window
on St. Valentine's,
and that real live chameleon
I sneaked out for you.
Remember when you climbed
up a rooftop to help down a mewling kitten,
the collapsing slates, you lying, winded,
asking for the kiss of life, and everybody laughing?

Hunters

They parcour on the wall between two streets.
The moon appears, picks out their silhouettes.
A short, sharp stink arouses all nearby.
The neighbours close their shutters, shrug and frown,
the night when Paris rings with yelping cats.
And some are black, some tigerishly striped,
their wailing walling in or walling out —
oh, just another urban mating game.
For other hunters it's an act of skill,
requiring stealth and silence, and no moon.
They move in darkness, while others sleep,
each claw extended, eye, vigilant.
If I could put a notion in his head,
he might track me, drag me to his bed.

Fin de Siècle

You feel hungry? Ask Godard;
he'll rustle up a piano, but expect blood.
And don't play with knives
in front of Betty,
she has an eye for them.
Who's to say several boys in mask
can't lick a cat into oblivion
or a river won't take two stones
along with a genius?

A Chinese lantern
goes lightly past the flame,
Fox into a new century.
And then there's God.
Give me fourteen minutes
and I'll tweak him out of you,
like Medusa's hairbrush snarl;
the monstrous backhander
wood gives in the dark.

I mean, your mother saw Laika;
she'd understand.
Haven't we indented
every groove with fingerprints
and bastardised the brushstrokes?
As for this downpour of starfish
in your wheelbarrow, plant them
in red waterbeds, before the director cuts
to a grenade on the porch.

Contact

'God and the Devil are one.'
    – Karen Blixen

I

Chopper's genuflection;
a *whoomph* disturbs the air.

Clansmen and women offer fruit;
a *whoomph* disturbs

a calabash, spills water;
a *whoomph*: white walls, a flare.

II

A mob; Kalashnikovs and rocks.
He cowers in a corner.

Hands seize
on splintered glass.

A looming face, teeth yellow-
stained from chewing *khat*

spring-loaded spittle
screaming hate.

III

The sea receives more bodies,
lays them on a beach.

Crossings lead
to razor wire, new fences.

IV

Boycotts and defences dance
like pirouettes, a paintbrush.

V

At an army base: 'I believe
he had no faith.'

The chaplain's agitated. 'But
we've got to say a prayer

before we zip the bag.
It's always been the way.'

Holy War

I

I lie on filthy straw, thumbs and fingers
circling my neck – width of a tender, fresh baguette.
To imagine it.

All I can hear is my blood. No bells or messages.
They call me traitor, heretic, idolater.
To recant, betray my Voices? Live?

II

The jailer produces my last dinner.
His spittle hits my face, as he jeers that it's not
to be the axe. I had imagined

a moment's judder over bone, then done.
Instead, my body is to be devoured by flames!
Oh, rather seven times the chop!

III

Memories keep returning,
like the revolutions of a wheel: grog-cheeks
and leers of courtiers, though I wore a soldier's tunic,

hose and doublet, hair a boyish crop.
Words erupted from a battle voice,
as though from elsewhere:

'My Lord, why let a mighty foreign hand
slope your shoulder, hold dominion!' Even as I spoke,
my father's scathing words returned to me:

How can you, a chit, believe
Almighty God has sent you to lead an army?
For such heresy, I will drown you, my own hands!

Yet, France roused herself and marched with me,
almost to the gates of victory! Fifty thousand men followed
my white banner, silver armour. I, the Voices.

IV

My eyes burn through the bars of this stinking dungeon.
All night, fear crawls across my skin.
How I dream, now, about my father's promised death!

Through thick stone walls, I hear the bells again,
lifting me beyond this earthly fear. Like death,
my faith is certain; and Paradise awaits!

Swordplay

You pare to get the closest zest,
find the sting back-lashing.
Oh I've been here before, shedding
skins till I was membrane thin
and boneless with compliance.
But we all need resistance:
no snap beneath the fingers
makes us bored. Well, I'm no
longer so domestic; you'll find
me less Siamese, more vixen.
I've been well taught – by one
who's always played to win;
find I like the thrust and cut,
and my skins have all grown back.

Slow Dancing in a Burning Room

If I follow footprints to a future memory,
I find you, lean and supple, though you blur a little.
That's because I'm pushing my heart
against you, and my eyes are mostly closed
to the squinting, bouncing dark.

It's the unknown
of the known that attracts me.
We move blindly around the room,
among the uninvited, and I drink you in,
as if through a straw, slowly, sucking deeply.

The others have departed
to be Martians, low gravity a safer bet
than burning. The doors, both back and front,
are still open, and the yellowwood floor is glowing.
Do we dim or brighten, before the sirens flare?

Leavings

On Receiving a Letter from a Soldier after his Death

i.m. N.B.

Every window shows a body
moving. A man pours from a jug.

Dead plants
on a balcony above water

rushing into trees.
A woman hastens in the half-light

to a capsized child
beneath a swing.

Leaves blink,
milk-green as a corpse.

Like the city, I am pressed,
again, again,

beneath the sky's broad palm,
its crushing weight.

Some Things are Hard to Shake Off

'These days,
only the Polish fill a church
on Good Friday.'

The music is sublime, so I slip in
to the memory
of habitual coughing,

watch children tripping up the aisle,
with pressed palms,
fresh as innocence

while the old remain in pews,
heads bent,
praying for buried friends,

and I find myself
saying the words again,
dipping my fingers

in holy water,
shaking them at something
behind me.

Giving Up the Ghost

As a child, I once hid
for a whole day in the rock field.
No one noticed my absence.

Now, I can't summon up
enough presence
to be witnessed.

In another country,
I'm interrupting
bath-time.

I avert my gaze.
'When you and John waltzed
together at our wedding,

I hoped for something like
that love,' he says, swirling
water with a soapy palm.

How I long for bone,
my husband's palm again,
against my spine!

He asks if I'd like to pass on
a message.
Tell John I'll be holding

his hand —the left one—
at the funeral,
but after, I'll be gone.

The first night my daughter
brought this young man home,
I urged her to marry him.

Another thing —
you must leave her, I manage.
You're both hurting.

Blink

They stream past me,
like phantom birds,
all the houses.

The first African one,
a hammerkop,
all messy crest;

another, a paradise fly-catcher;
the third, a heron.
Sometimes they brush

the edge of wild bush,
or a silvery river,
warming their tails

in the sun, till the vanishing.
One for each year
of a migratory childhood.

Long corridors, tall steps,
cold rooms, glass roofs.
Across a hemisphere,

some standing on lawns,
bright as sugar,
dressed up,

like mannequins,
temporary playthings
before another re-crossing.

Tucked at the end
of a long cul-de-sac,
one comes close

to what you'd call home:
close enough to look into the glossy
pellet of a sun-struck eye,

see the malachite-amber blur.
But it slips
through my fingers,

and once again I am left
with nothing
but a flickering.

Leavings

Even in cities,
there are places to be alone,
with drizzle and roses
in a late evening park,
clouds bulging above,
beds nestled,
and paths,
where I walk,
hands reading stone walls,
overgrown bushes, brackish and green,
the ground sucking and squelching,
occasional tree-flap of a crow,
a lone dog sniffing at trees…
no – not alone after all.

The whizz-light of five o'clock traffic,
cryptic Morse flashing, like questions
asking for something other
than customary consolations.
There are benches.
I sit, waiting for answers;
for the come-and-go comfort of another
headlight taking a bend in the distance.
Then it's back to the kissing
darkness again, and silence.
A strand of hair in my mouth,
knees pressed together,
the drip and trickle moments,
plural as memory.

La Rue du Chat qui Pêche

Rain turns up its music.
Confetti

for a monkey wedding.
Not worth wearing a helmet.

He lights up, stares
down the skinny alley.

Gamine arrives on a bicyclette;
paper-clipped skirt.

Stops beside his scooter.
In her basket, pantone tarts.

Blurred light overlaps the plume
she slices with a finger.

Last glimmerings
of a purple sky.

'She's still at the corner,
making crêpes,

the one with the warty cheek.'
But where's the cat?

Shadow

(after Hans Christian Anderson)

Why is she so uncertain?
Since her big decision
to move to the sun,
I've become the shadow
of a phantom! In the evening,
instead of curling about her feet
as becomes a shadow,
I climb up the walls!

The windows are high and open
and on the balcony across
the lawn, a stranger releases
a musky pheromone.
I crawl across the railing,
each evening reaching further
away from her, towards
the body of the world.

One night, a catapulting leap,
and I am torn. Oh, I can't
tell her how I've discovered
passion's bounty, a lover's tongue,
while she sits, so solitary,
bitten thin from lack!
Yet, out of pity, I return
with an invitation.

Deluge

The purple sky's being felled, like skittles
with a crow bar, ice skitter-skattering,
and all you can do is swim through the storm

orbiting abandoned love and tomorrows,
while through an open door, steam from the chipper
rises into an empty street, and farther down,

old people are heaving furniture-boats into the river
already filled with adventurous boys,
whose mothers are crying over letters left behind;

and you hear the rumble of hundreds of feet tumbling
down a staircase somewhere, and glasses are flying, like bats,
cracking into obstacles as you run, angling elbows

against the wave that appears in the doorway, an overflowing raft,
and you reach a trapdoor, where a cat's being stripped of flesh
and eaten raw by assassins in teen clothing.

Now all that's left is somniphobia, loose floorboards
and one last egg, still hidden
in the kind darkness of a salvaged handbag.

Precipitation

Small dramas of rain,
ribboning swathes,
like a woman's sorrows, multiplying.

Each soaking night, her heart in an uproar.
She remembers his hands gesturing,
like a mathematician's, in skilled division.

Recurring images, Good Friday guilt,
anguish toppling weekly,
into her handkerchief pocket.

She thinks of the mouth she kissed;
the mudflat drawl,
so profane, enticing.

She keeps the part of him that loved
to dance; his languorous arms,
as she casually gave her virginity.

After some years, her mind changes
direction, rain shifting
at last to the west.

But how near, sometimes,
she is in the dark. The rain sees it all,
one wave after another, striking the rock.

Cat's eye stars, sleep-in hours.
She wonders if, during the weather,
he still remembers.

Or Perhaps

I

A woman sits before a picture window.
On the table in front of her,
The Crimson Petal and the White.
She stares out across the garden.
A cradled cat rubs insistently against her wrist.
Eventually, the wrist twitches.
She narrows her eyes at the grass's
sharp blades, pointing.
Her phone shudders on the table,
crashes to the floor.
A faint movement of her mouth.

II

A man, whose head is shaved, pacing.
He manipulates his hands, one after the other,
lays a two-palmed cap across his skull,
holding still the bony, sensitive exterior.
His eyes dissect the driveway.
Hanging in his mouth, a pair of names,
lips uncertain which to choose.
The grasses wave their swords,
as though challenging the wind to blow them over.
Or perhaps they are listening for a name.

Cold Air Awakening

Call Up

From toy soldiers out of tins,
to khaki in the trunk,

from surfing out of barrels,
to three bullets in a bag.

Come on boys, be brothers
to each other and the wind:

outrun the warring shadows
of mercenary old men!

Sonnet in B Major

Sway, everybody.
Even the horse that shies, the child on paper,
drawing. Green-easy, until flummoxed.
Do magic, like feral creatures turning
quick to a language, cold air awakening.
Coins are still legitimate, but not quiet anymore.
A wet black semi-quaver opening up
the frantic eye of an arbitrary Icarus.
Oh, these bells. But I digress.
If we must die, ingloriously, let's first
rise up like snakes from the monumental pit.
We don't get back for a second year.
Speed's got a nerve, a no-time, strident
bunch of followers. All these criminal acts?
Move the iceberg, or lose the Titanic, everything.

Flight MH370

And a crack in the teacup opens
in the lane to the land of the dead.

—WH Auden

Expressions stare inwards.
Some faces press
against ovals of panes,
as the aeroplane hastens
into radar silence.
Under that blanket, a boy
is counting time on his fingers.
A girl sleeps against
her mother's unmoving
shoulder, while she soars away,
thoughts exploding.
Some frantically ask questions.
Two hundred and thirty nine passengers,
texting those precious three words.
A man takes the hand of a stranger
beside him, holds on
to loneliness.
Touch will keep him feeling
alive, until the last moment.
She doesn't pray,
but thinks of drinking rum
with those fishermen
in Kuching, the music,
everybody laughing.

L'Esprit d'Escalier

I

Flossie, let's put the bomb inside the Trojan horse.
Our lives are just coffee tables, tattered rugs.
We could find the velvet beneath new petals.
Your smile, that cherry lipstick – way, oh!
When I say let's, between words and words,
flesh might be outraged. But I promise not to go
into twittersphere, all that gibberish. This is just
to say, Flossie, I love your alabaster skin.

II

Al, a snake rising repeatedly
is only to be mocked
for its dandruff and over-shiny shoes.
The only bitter I'll consider
is dark chocolate grated over a lemon
drizzle cake, made by the skinniest man
this side of the lush carpet (who has more than words
in his seduction closet).

III

Ah, Flossie, cut me some slack.
Give me the late afternoons, low thumping
inside your ribs. It's good to stand at the top of the stairs
for a different view. Maybe Instagram, though on the whole,
I prefer to keep away from social media.
I don't sleep much, hyper-kinetic, perhaps, or this:
the way electric currents animate the rose under your skin.
What else could we blow up?

IV

Al, long before you mentioned bombs in horses,
you began the death throes.
Oh, you smile, but at the corners of your eyes, I look for daggers.
You may as well ask me to emigrate
to Mars with a preacher man.
I see you for what you are, your small game.
Which is to say, your fishing line
will never reach so much as a threat of water.

Holocene

Wolf rain,
dragging down the mountain

or kinetic,
beating up the alley wall

or bad friend,
electrocuting streets

or, slipping, like cat-fur
from your shoulders

or slant-subversive
against a torso

or rain that addresses you
with violence

spear-thrown,
from Zulu skies

or a glacial rebound,
copper-threaded

or thick,
like vertebrae

or sliding, like liquorice,
down a throat

or composed, like wine,
full-bodied

or body-bagged,
ready for a requiem.

The Man who Fell from the Sky

i.m. José Matada

Small and black,
like a fleck in the eye;

arms flung out
in a Moro reflex.

Passersby stopped
in their tracks,

transfixed by the minor
sideshow

of death.
One boy would not

look down,
watched instead

as a pale yellow sun
lifted

into the sky
as though it were flying.

I Is Not Always Me

'Je est un autre'
  —Arthur Rimbaud

I take four trains each way, through bleary light.
Hide from the city noise inside my head,
where there's only silence, or the memory of her cello.
My blood's grown thick; my body moves more slowly.
That first day, some racist in a drive-by aimed an egg.
It hit my back. He chased the car, caught up
at the lights and threw a punch.
The stairwell to our bedsit reeks with piss.

Hall is crammed with bicycles.
Once, I cycled to the river, sat all day and stared.
Pebbles. Floating foliage. Strange fish.
He roared at me when I returned,
thought he'd have to have it dredged.
Holds me when I wail at night.
I miss my mother. He tells me
to pretend she's dead.

They come from everywhere, the others:
Syria, Peru, Fiji, Senegal.
Today we look at colours. Our teacher gestures
to the window, but of course, the sky is rarely blue.
I'm an immigrant, she says, *like you*.
And this – she points to the screen, a southern ocean –
THIS is blue. She tells us about blue movies,
how blue's also an emotion.

In Advanced, we talk about erosion,
cliffs giving way, landing in the sea.
I think of how a foreign language percolates
your own, until its idioms even permeate your dreams.
That's not just acquisition, but erosion too.
It's only when I follow the slow river,
and the first real sun of summer
kisses fire to its skin, that I remember.

Tea with Tiresias

'My dear, I'm wearing my Mexican cravat
for your benefit! Am I not resplendent?
Come, give me a hug, let me take
your coat. Now settle on the sofa, right here beside me,
have some tea. I'm going blind, I suppose
they've told you. Do you mind if I touch
your lovely face and shoulders, clavicle,
the swelling of...yes, well now, here's the cat.

She was spayed, just recently,
poor little thing, so wounded. I gave her
solace on my knee, stroked until she purred.
Have you just come back from Africa?
I remember, in Johannesburg, seeing a knife-fight
between two women, one stabbed, and squealing like a pig.
Like a pig! Then she darted into traffic...oh dear...
they always shake, my fingers, take no notice.

I'm trying to figure out if you remarried.
Ah. You're not telling! Très mystérieuse.
You're very warm. Of course you're young.
I'm ashamed to say I'm seventy five, or thereabouts.
Perhaps a decade older. And what have I done?
What left to look forward to?
Don't mention writing or reflection.
I've no time for that. My thoughts are elsewhere.

So soon?
Here, let me hug you. Forgive the tears.
Kiss me on both cheeks, like a continental.
I can tell you this:
you'll never lose your hot blood.
Let me see you to the porch –
oh such chilly wind, so dark,
and now this rain! Must you really go?'

The Glass Delusion

When I was a boy, I told my mother
about strange things that I dreamt.
Translucent wings leaping from my shoulders.
The sun, a liquid furnace in my mouth.
Glass trees erupting from my feet.
She said, 'You're an artist.'
What fire bellowed into me
with that pronouncement! Like hothouses
growing beyond the neighbours' walls,
they started to appear: crystal snakes, goblets,
colossal rainbow globes.

Then one day, at the entrance steps, I crashed
into my new neighbour, who picked me up,
offered me some quince. In her room,
she mocked my fumbling virginity.
I'm convinced there was some sorcery,
because here I am, in front
of every mirror, locked in!
All this new matter, risk of tripping,
falling, breaking into smithereens.
Last night I dreamt I was sitting, as you are,
step-like, in that armchair, by the fire.

The terror of that dream! How can I bend my knees?
I must paint like this, encased in iron ribs, for protection,
my arm extended in a brace, then lowered
by this pulley, when I need to sleep.
All day and night, my heart, a bird of glass,
thuds its frantic wings against my chest!
Even more unendurable, are eyes that gaze
so freely at my every wheeling thought.
Such shadowless transparency!
Or perhaps, though you see right through me,
like the glass in that window, I remain invisible?

Pareidolia

Near the estuary, silt xylophones
over shale and pebble,
calibrated fossils.

Flotsam for a paleontologist:
a skull's tumultuous
possibilities.

Loping up the hill, a fresh wind,
its visible list across a green swathe
shaping into an entwined couple.

Hallucinations create
their own inflections.
Limewashed, spiralling clouds,

atolls that curl, yellow, violet, blue,
like a magician's legerdemain
handkerchief, bright as the light

of a toppling coin. A lone glider.
Pilot plays dare, larks
about in the palace sky

eyes the arc
of the sun, in the silent moment
before its plummet.

A Matter of Persistence

'Out of such persistence arose turtles, rivers,
mitochondria, figs…'
— Jane Hirshfield

Bleary aftermath of rain, the endless pressing feet.
Two lads lean against a wall.
The alley smokes with river mist.
From behind this sudden curtain, a ghost
cat dreams of returning to the city.

The living squall, piss along the granite.
There's no denying it: she no longer dances
on the pavement; emits no heat or scent.
But she persists, for days and decades,
until this evening's new constellation – lynx –

or certain slant of streetlight, lifts her gaze –
and it begins – a ripple, right across her painted coat!
Just an illusion, scoffs the taller one
to his staring friend. Then, right in front of him,
the mural disappears.

Next thing, he sees a frisson becoming
solid in the street; a bristling, vivid, green-eyed
density, with every double-take!
His disbelief is stalled
when she caterwauls, tail a victory flag.

Particle of light
in a raindrop

Scratch

A cat scratch, I tell the waitress
when she touches my wrist.
'Who won?'

I laugh, show her all my scars.
A man walks by, soused in rain.
Then someone lifts a saxophone.

For as long as he plays, you sit
across from me, my long-
remaindered intimate,

until a whistling draught flies me
back to my solitude. A kind
of coupling, my freedom and this.

Whoosh

for Micaela

Dust blurs the image.
I brush my thumb across the frame.
You hold a rod; you're half my height.

With every passing year,
you grow more
mysterious, my love.

Hot air balloons float across my journal.
A dedication: 'Thank you for being
the best mum in the known universe.'

The baskets hang above a quilt
of snowy cumulus.
I imagine standing in the front one.

Hear the hiss.
Blustering all around me,
seven massive onions.

To think,
a hemisphere away, you're
in the thick of a different season's day.

Soon, this chilly black will become
more ashen, sharpen objects.
Before light

and reason reach,
I let myself be – whooshed! –
across two continents

to your garden.
Quick – intrepid birds will soon
be landing on the wires

and twittering.
But first, let me land this
mighty, striped balloon; a kiss!

Ghost of the Fisher Cat

How do describe the topography
of the imagination?
Let's start with that fish,

lying in the gutter,
brought up from the river, or myth.
Phew, the whiff!

Go on, observe
for yourself: glinting in the rain,
silver as a metal grid.

Like fauna between glacial layers,
twilight need offer nothing
more than the power

of imagination – this trophy
from a ghost cat's watery skirmishes,
for example.

So perfect, it could almost
be a feat of taxidermy.
Don't stare.

Let your eyes go soft;
sense peripherals,
like an animal tracker.

See? There she goes!
The cat, her sinuous spring, back
into the shadows.

You didn't catch her?
Well, there are always losses and gains,
as with any fishing expedition.

It requires a certain leap of your own
to jump out of one world
and into another.

It's All Material

'She's stroking her cat,
and the skin on her arms
is mottled, quite old,
with dark patches, like oil
spilled on wood.
And she's talking
about prisoners
and shadows
on walls in a cave.
I pull out my notebook,
casually, like.
"Oh, *Plato* – right,"
I say, as I write,
'*cheetah skin.*'

The Importance of Being

'Who can calculate the orbit of his own soul?'
— Oscar Wilde

Today is mineral, a swathe
of rain slanting

through the branches
of birches, shivering firs.

He imagines the clean bright
droplets on his tongue,

bells in his ear, birds
flittering all around him.

Each reflection
takes him far beyond

these four-walled days,
floats his soul

through this tiny window,
into illumination.

Alchemy of Happiness
for Cian

A half-wild boy, panting up the hill
under a cyan sky, cloud-ragged.
His body asks a question, gives an answer.

Mosaics of light, like a secret,
are captured in this song of slanted movement:
a half-wild boy, panting up the hill.

His urge to run leaps from foot to foot,
and earth exhales its pleasure in response.
His body asks a question, gives an answer.

The chill wind swings behind him, like
memories shaken out, snapped laundry.
A half-wild boy panting up the hill.

He flies through doorless rooms,
across a private ocean, to a pinnacle.
His body asks a question, gives an answer.

Each day's discovery, a kind of grace.
Arms winged above his head, a stork, uplifting.
A half-wild boy, panting on the hill.
His body asks a question, gives an answer.

In Sunlight

(after Ilya Kaminsky)

Imaginary balconies seek fifty poplars,
and they blame sunlight; the body shooting,
an arrogant earth, sunlight falling by the man
on Tedna St; one becomes a sunlight pair,
learns scissors in a week, and the fourteenth
horse cuts his mouth there, and they sat down,
shot sunlight to us today;
                       all body things
seek a girl, a boy, no hair in our shoes,
on lips, a school from the live body world;
say sunlight, girl; speak in sunlight, boy;
write of a girl, tell women, and I know,
what man does not, for when a child steals
sunlight, they, with sunlight on hair – a girl
putting sunlight on her lips – is what I was,
just I, within you, inside sunlight.

Almost, but Never, the Truth

'I wasn't good at childhood,'
you say. 'Somehow,
that led me into art.'
My eyes pan
from a gold-leaf torso,
made from glass,
to ancient maritime charts.
Maybe there is a message.

The present is already past
by the time words are out
of your mouth. You shoot
the air with the serum of ideas;
tell me what you heard
in the rainy street –
'flowers will drink
almost anything' –

as you draw the drapes,
select a rioja: Luis Cañas.
One wall is bare.
You say white space
is for inspiration,
like Schiller's rotten apples.
I drink, as I do in charged up
mood or weather.

Bolder now. We don't
have oceans of time.
'Would you put up
a Picasso with two noses?'
You laugh, then show me
the real story.
Between your teeth,
a tongue, hibiscus-pink.

Ode to an Itinerant Cat

You've begun to follow me home.
Aren't strays usually found in alleys and quays?
At the late-night bus stop, aren't you the fleet shadow?

Père Lachaise catacombs have a few too.
I'll bet they are within your radius; can see you communing
with ghosts. Your harlequin eyes have their secrets.

I've heard that cats are the ultimate alchemists, comforters
for the ill and forgetful, attendants at elsewheres.
No wonder, for some, cats are sacred.

I'm still cautious – your moods shift in an instant,
from winding round ankles to spit, dagger eyes and dromedary
hackles, tail a flickering warning. But we're getting there.

And now, here: my almost-familiar – it's taken a year –
slipping at last into my lap, like rain-spill into a river,
your purring, electric as fences, vibrating through skin.

Notes

The cover on this book is credited to a graffiti artist identified as Némo. It depicts the cat of an urban myth on the narrowest street in Paris: *Rue du Chat qui Pêche*. According to the legend, in the 15th century, a canon, by the name of Dom Perlet, lived on this tiny street with his enormous black cat, who frequented the banks of the Seine, often appearing to catch a fish with one swipe of his mighty paw. The fact that Dom Perlet was also an alchemist led those who were superstitious to believe that the pair were involved in witchcraft. Three young vigilantes took it upon themselves to drown the cat in the Seine. Mysteriously, the alchemist also vanished – for a while. Around the same time that Perlet returned, the cat reappeared, and continued fishing.

Sadly, the mural has since been removed.

Information from https://studiosparis.wordpress.com/tag/la-rue-du-chat-qui-peche/

*

The title 'Vital impulse' is after Henri Bergson's *'élan vital'*.

'1606 Round-up' refers to the round-up of Irish immigrants in Paris in that year, to be returned by ship to Ireland.

'...*lors que sur la Seine on embarqua les Irlandois pour les renvoyer chez eux, leur ordonnant & distribuant vous même les vivres & provisions pour la commodité de leur voyage.*'

('..so that when the Irish embark on the Seine to be returned home, food and provisions should be ordered & distributed by yourselves for the convenience of their journey.')
    —Bellièvre letter at the Bibliothèque Nationale de Paris (BNF)

*

'Contact' is inspired by a scene in Angus Shaw's non-fiction book, 'Mutoko Madness'. The image 'a pirouette, a paintbrush' makes reference to the open letter exchange between Mia Oudeh and JK Rowling.

*

The epigraph in 'Leap' refers to Homer Simpson's observation after Lisa creates a machine whose heat and energy *increase* with time.

*

In 'Hunters', I use the French word 'parcour', which translates as 'free running', preferring this to the somewhat ugly English spelling, 'parkour'.

*

'Slow Dancing in a Burning Room' is the title of a song by John Mayer.

*

In 'Or Perhaps', reference is made to *The Crimson Petal and the White*, a novel by Michel Faber.

*

'Glass Delusion': According to Gill Speak, in *History of Psychiatry*, from 1440 to 1705, there were many cases of people who suffered from the delusion that they were made of glass, which was a relatively new material at the time.

*

'It's All Material' references Plato's well-known Allegory of the Cave.

*

The poem, 'In Sunlight', is a remix of Ilya Kaminsky's 'Fourteenth Week' and includes every word in the original poem.

Photograph by Toma McCullim

AFRIC MCGLINCHEY's début collection, *The lucky star of hidden things*, was published by Salmon Poetry, and features a number of poems set in Zimbabwe, where she was raised. The collection was translated into Italian and work has also been translated into Spanish, Irish, and Polish. Her awards include a Hennessy Emerging Poetry Award, the Northern Liberties Poetry Prize (USA), Poets meet Politics Prize and a Faber Academy fellowship. She has read at international festivals including the Poetry Africa Festival, the Harare International Festival of the Arts, Troubadour London, the Benedict Kiely Festival in Northern Ireland and Paris Live, as well as throughout Ireland. She was one of the writers selected for the Italo-Irish Literature Exchange in 2014, with readings in Rome, Bologna, Lugo and St Agata. Afric was Poet in Residence at the Uillinn: West Cork Arts Centre for four months and was awarded a Cork County Council arts bursary in 2015. Afric has been selected as one of Ireland's Rising poets by Poetry Ireland Review. She lives in West Cork. www.africmcglinchey.com